Fragrant Fields

Poetic Reflections for Journaling

by Kathryn Ross

*May Fragrant Fields
of Blessings be yours!
Kathryn Ross
Psalm 45:1*

Pageant
Wagon
Publishing
Family Literacy Books

Fragrant Fields: Poetic Reflections for Journaling
Written by Kathryn Ross
Cover and Interior Design by Kathryn Ross

ISBN: 978-0-9981771-2-0

Pageant Wagon Publishing © 2005, 2017
A Division of Pageant Wagon Productions LLC
www.pageantwagonpublishing.com
info@pageantwagonpublishing.com

Dedication

For my husband, Ed—
the "he" to my "she"
—the other side of me;
a selfless servant
to my writer's reverie,
and constant support
in all my creative endeavors.
God blessed me with a loving helpmeet
who has stood by me through the years,
never doubting,
always trusting,
deeply enriching,
my efforts towards
the printed page.

Table of Contents

Introduction

Poets, like artists, have the gift of helping us
see and hear what we might pass by.

Rosalie Slater

The day starts like any other day: copious errands to run, children to shuttle about, meals to prepare, a time clock to punch. The daily grind.

I wonder what use my cozy little house with the cottage décor, comfy reading chair surrounded by bookshelves, and fragrant front rose garden is to me, when I spend the better part of my days charging about in my car, rushing from job, to grocery store, to the mall, to appointment what-nots, checking each off my endless list of things to do.

Introverted me craves time for Retreat and Reflection so all my busy might be glazed in the sweetness of Rest and Renewal. But, too often Urgent overwhelms Important. Retreat, Reflection, Rest, and Renewal are relegated to the least of my priorities. I feel a sense of loss in the void.

I ponder this, chastening my innermost being as I race my daughter to her friend's pool party. The unfamiliar road has the ambience of a charming country retreat setting. I silently snatch a whiff of the atmosphere whizzing past, seizing restful thoughts on the go.

I think: *What a nice job they did with their landscaping over there. How quaint to fill one's front yard with bird houses next block down. Oh, look! That bunny scampered out of the way of my wheels just in time.*

1

*Snippets of beauty and nature have such scope
for Retreat . . . for Romance, even.*

But, I need more than a snippet—and am about to get my fill. Today, I'm on a collision course with God's grace. As I round a curve, Jesus meets me face to face. Immediately I am the prodigal, returned, hungry and hopeful for a feast and a fatted calf.

What I get is poetry. Actually—a field.

A huge expanse. Yards and yards of purple lavender and golden wildflowers sway in the soft summer breeze. Distant emerald green trees form a dramatic backdrop, offset by the brilliance of a sapphire sky. The scene shouts from heaven an emphatic, *"Stop! It is good!"* I see and hear, but am forced to pass it by.

"Mother! Watch the road!" My daughter is quick to nudge me back to the business at hand. Yes, we are almost there. Safely depositing my seventeen-year-old for an afternoon swim, I purpose to return to that little wisp of Eden on an unfamiliar lane.

There, I pull to the roadside and sit, drinking in the wonder of God's Creation. Hues of purple, gold, green, and blue dazzle my eyes. The "buzz" of bumble-bees performing their God-ordained act of worship amongst the wildflowers tickle my ears. My nose twitches at the scent of lavender and clover. I'm captured by an irresistible urge to take off running, in all abandon, through the floral sea before me.

Then—I think of ticks. And how I'm wearing the wrong shoes. And what a fool I would look to the neighbor across the street. How I envy his living room view.

Abandon withdrawals to its convenient cage, rather than become a tangible reality. The cares of this world bully my desire to worship. Unrestrained. I feel the twinge of shame. The sting of Regret. A resolve towards Repentance swells from deep within and I determine to return to this spot with my husband. I want to share the Beauty of the Lord and the fleeting moment of worship I've experienced in this place with him.

We do return, my husband and me. With camera in hand. We exclaim at the greatness of our God and the marvel of His works. Two of us are gathered—and in His midst. No, I don't run through the floral sea. It is not for me to intrude upon the landscape. I'm on holy ground—perhaps I ought to take off my shoes. The awe of the moment is meat and wine enough. I hear the voice of my Lord and am satisfied. But desire more.

God, in His gentle way, uses those few stolen moments by the side of Busy to cause me to crave longer stays in our trysting place. Through the years, we've carved out many "secret places" of worship much like that fragrant field. Seeds of inspiration are planted there, coming to fruition after a brooding season. Then, in cloistered moments with pen and paper, keyboard and screen, I flood my Response through the written word.

Poems. Prose. Story. Drama.

Some places are mere moments. Others—hours, days, seasons. They are emblazoned in my spirit in the photo album of my mind—a God encounter in my most intimate zone.

Retreat. Reflection. Rest. Renewal. Romance. Restoration.

Inspired by that fragrant field I've harvested here a sampling, spanning some thirty-plus years, of musings and journal records, collected literary quotes, and life Scriptures. From the tender, naïve love poems of my youth, when I did not know the Lord—though He knew me—to the grown-up voice of life experience, and the fruit of meditations in God's Word.

These poems, stories, and journal prompts chronicle bumpy roads well-traveled, learning the way of faith, truth, and the steadfast love of God in my life, as I seek to *"see and hear what others may pass by."*

For instance, I composed *Wings* at the impressionable age of fourteen. Other writings are excerpts from plays I've written and produced. Some passages were lyrics for songs, while others were dramatized performance pieces. *Letter to a Hopeless Romantic* is a redraft of an actual letter I wrote to a young girl I once mentored—an appendix to another teenage love poem lamenting loss. I wrote it as an exhortation to her in a critical period of growth. I was about to move away and feared for her heart. Would she look to God alone to be the Lover of her soul?

Fragrant Fields is a small slice of my devotional life shared to inspire contemplatives in reflective journaling. Follow the expanded thoughts and writing prompts when you see the icon of a book and pen.

Metaphors abound. Dig deeply. Chew slowly. This is the Retreat and Reflection part, producing the Rest and Renewal part, leading to the Romantic part. And Restoration.

But it's up to you to complete the beauty of poetic Reflection in your own unique Response as you pause on holy ground—not to me as the poet, but to God, the Ultimate Author, Light, and Lover of your soul.

Be blessed and be a blessing . . .

Kathryn Ross
Vineland, New Jersey
January 2017

4

On the Telling of Stories

A good story is a compass
Pointing my imagination
In diverse directions.
I set sail on a raft of rhymes and reasons
Plumbing the depths of man's heart,
And rise-up on waves of virtue triumphant
Where I see a fixed mark on the horizon.
It is there that I know
To set my rudder and my sails,
Sure to the breeze,
In the hope of docking safely
On the shoreline
Of a firm foundation
For life and living.

Jesus always used stories and illustrations like these when speaking to the crowds. In fact, he never spoke to them without using such parables. This fulfilled what God had spoken through the prophet:
"I will speak to you in parables.
I will explain things hidden since the creation of the world."

Matthew 13:34-35 NLT

Do a study on the following words using the *Noah Webster's 1828 Dictionary of the American English Language*, available online at: webstersdictionary1828.com

NOTE: The *1828 Dictionary* is the fruit of twenty years of research by Noah Webster, defining words from a biblical, classical, historical perspective, as used and understood by the founding generations of the United States. Think and reason through the definition of these terms and review the verses of the poem with greater depth and insight. Apply this method throughout your poetic reading and writing in this book by choosing key words to define and ponder. Write your thoughts.

Compass	Plumb	Virtue
Fixed	Rudder	Docking
Firm	Foundation	Life

 Is there a Bible story in either the Old Testament or New Testament that has a particularly special place in your heart? Why? Do you see yourself in the story? How? Write about it in your journal.

 Is there a Parable that Jesus told which has served as a compass to set your rudder to dock "safely on the shore of a firm foundation for life and living?" Write about it in your journal.

O my people, listen to my instructions.
Open your ears to what
I am saying,
for I will speak to you in a parable.
I will teach you hidden lessons
from our past—
stories we have heard and known,
stories our ancestors
handed down to us.
We will not hide these truths
from our children;
we will tell the next generation
about the glorious deeds of the Lord,
about his power
and his mighty wonders.

Psalm 78:1-4 NLT

Cloistered

Look! Sapphire Skies.
Listen! Seaside Sounds.
Feel! Whirling Winds.
Smell! Fragrant Fields.
Taste! Plentiful Plantations

The splendor of Creation—Speaks.

Rejoice! Melodic Moments.
Revel! Stirring Stories.
Reflect! Wondering Words
Retreat! Pastoral Places.

In His Contemplative Presence—Renewed.

Cloistered
In all intimacy and abandon.
A place of awed speechlessness
Yet dynamic response.
A realm of surrender beyond definition.
Dare we thrust open the garden gate and commune with
our Beloved among the roses?
Dare we pass the threshold of our comfort zone
And consume it to ashes with His Intimate Zone?
Speaking and spoken to
I am known—and I know Him.
I am my Beloved's and my Beloved is mine.

The heavens proclaim the glory of God.
The skies display his craftsmanship.
Day after day they continue to speak;
night after night they make him known.
They speak without a sound or word;
their voice is never heard.
Yet their message has gone throughout the
earth, and their words to all the world.
Psalm 19:1-4 NLT

Beautiful words stir my heart.
I will recite a lovely poem about the king,
for my tongue is like the pen of a skillful poet.
Psalm 45:1 NLT

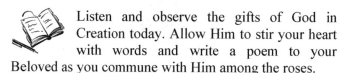These are just two of my "life verses" in the Scriptures that have informed my devotional life. Listening to the Voice of God in Creation inspires a deep understanding of His character as revealed in His written Word—the Bible; and living Word—Jesus. Responding with my own words—poetic words—I write and recite as prayer to my King. Even if my skill pales the masters and are more the scribbled love notes of a small child, they are His joy. What parent doesn't cherish such treasures! Write out one or two of your "life verses" from God's Love Letter, the Bible, and tell why they are so precious to you.

Listen and observe the gifts of God in Creation today. Allow Him to stir your heart with words and write a poem to your Beloved as you commune with Him among the roses.

Poets, musicians, artists—these who speak words of
beauty, play notes of glory, paint pictures of wonder.
Haley Richardson

Sing, Heavenly Muse . . .

I now invoke Thine aid . . .

Thou, O Spirit that does prefer

Before all Temples

the pure and upright heart,

Instruct me, for Thou knowest;

Thou from the first

Was present, and,

with mighty wings outspread,

Dovelike sat brooking

on the vast Abyss

What is dark in me

Illumine, what is low,

Raise and support.

John Milton
Paradise Lost, Book 1

13

Seaside Muse

Sun
Sky
Water
Sparkling water
Electric!

Bedazzled in Light
From shoreline to horizon
The longer I stare
Lost in the tinsel-twinkle
The more the sparks fly
Leaping
Skipping
Dancing
Wildly alive and luminous
Radiant!

Rolling at last
Onto the rocks
Licking my feet
I'm ignited
Set aflame!
By Living Water

The current rises
Surges through my body
Energy animates
Death to Life
Dark to Light
I sparkle bright
Like the sea
Energized!
By the Light of the Lord

And should I stay
Mesmerized—staring
Steadily out to sea
From the shore

The surf ripples
Rushes!
Ever closer from the deep
Whitecaps spray
They spatter me
Then swathe me
The flood tides
Your shimmering swells
Charged with Light
Seek me out
I have naught but to wait
You'll come to me
Saturated
I will be
Everyday
In the pulse of Your ebb and flow
Left in Your wake
I consider
The treasures deposited
By Your waves ablaze

MUSE *n.*

> Properly, song; but in usage, the deity or
> power of poetry . . . the genius of poetry.
>
> *v.* To ponder; to think closely; to study in
> silence; to wonder
> *I muse on the works of thy hands.* Psalms 143:5

Noah Webster's 1828 Dictionary

Ponder This: Have you ever seen water electrified? It is a deadly combination—water and electricity. Both can kill, and both can raise to life: Water renewing the parched body, dehydrated and dying; electrical shocks to restart a stopped heart and renew a body to live again.

The day I wrote this poem, I sat, solitary, in an Adirondack chair on a rocky shoreline, staring out over the sea under the sun. Listening. I heard the waves roll. Ebb and flow. But it was what I saw when I took the time to look. Electricity sparkling on the ripples of water. Words flowed through my pen to my journal. The moment and imagery, the sensation of the breeze gently caressing my skin—this treasure deposited that day is an eternal gift no human force can ever steal away. My Lord and me communing by the sea.

 Write about a treasured moment the Lord deposited into your Experience Box. Work to find the most descriptive words possible. Use language tools like the *1828 Dictionary* or a Thesaurus. Roll the words around and around as you dig deep to make an indelible marker of this love-moment shared between you and the Lord. What did you learn of Him? What did you learn of yourself?

Come, Holy Spirit, fill the hearts of Thy faithful
And enkindle them, with the fires of Thy love;
Send forth thy Spirit, and they shall be created,
And Thou shalt renew the face of the earth.

Book of Common Prayer

Rendezvous de Coeur

the music
the lyric
the dance
the drama
the style
the color
the substance
the pageantry
the quiet
the passionate word

these transports
cross the threshold of our inmost being
reach beyond personality and preference
captivate the place all men share in common

as the spoon stirs the pot
vegetables and meat swirl to the soup's surface

so too the vehicles of human expression
possess a God ordained power
to raise from the depths
our secret self
we awake
a soul spirited
God's desired dwelling place from the dawn of Creation
His Temple within a fragile human border
a secret chamber
to meet with His Redeemed
in all intimacy—and abandon
a place of awed speechlessness
yet dynamic response
a realm of surrender beyond definition
a place within ourselves too often walled up
guarded
perhaps forgotten
ignored

Speak, Art!
Declare, Beauty!
Spin your tales, Bard!
Awake! Persuade! Inspire!

 Ponder This: Art strengthens any message communicated with persuasive power. It cuts to the heart of its audience. Artistic expression, layered one on another, such as written words, sung, with musical accompaniment, interpreted through dance, on a dressed stage, intensifies the potency of the message communicated, capturing heart and mind. We must be careful to discern messages so adorned—be they meet for saving or slavery.

Reflective thinking is the key to reading and understanding poetry, an art form which demands one to STOP! And think about it. "Selah" is a Hebrew word used throughout the Psalms—the poetry book of the Bible—meaning just that. Re-read the poems and "selah." Journal about your personal experience with a poem, novel, musical composition, drama, or artistic expression as it relates to the themes in *Rendezvous de Coeur*.

Consider this Longfellow verse:

God sent His Singers upon earth
With songs of sadness and of mirth
That they might touch the hearts of men,
And bring them back to heaven again.
                    Henry Wadsworth Longfellow

Who are the "Singers" God has sent to the earth? Why

do they sing songs of both sadness and happiness? How does art, music, and poetry touch your heart—your innermost being?

 English poet, Robert Browning wrote:

*"God Himself is the best Poet,
and the Real is His song."*

Explain how the "Real" of God's poetry and song can bring our hearts "back to Heaven."

 Write your thoughts on the following quote from Eugene Peterson, as he comments in the *Conversations Bible* on *"doing the will of My Father"* in Matthew 7:24:

. . . from the Greek "poieō" which in other translations is rendered "do" . . . which is a very active word, we get the English word "poet." A poet is a person who takes words and does something with them, makes something personal and original out of them. Jesus says, "Be poets. Make something of these words I've spoken to you. Make a life, epic and poetic. And make it beautiful. Make it a work of art." That's something we can all do. One well-chosen word at a time. One stanza of service at a time. And with our words and deeds, we can leave something beautiful behind in the lives of others.

 To *poieō*, crafting action words that are works of art reflecting Truth, requires the daily exercise of both *selah* and *seeing* in depth. Poets who help others to *"see and hear what they might pass by"* make the deliberate effort to not just see—but observe. Look. Deeper. Write your thoughts on how you distinguish between seeing and observing.

You see, but you do not observe. The distinction is clear.
Sir Arthur Conan Doyle
Sherlock Holmes—*A Scandal in Bohemia*

There is not a form that lives in the world,
but is a window cloven through the blank
darkness of nothingness, to let us look into
the heart, and feeling, and nature of God.

This world is not merely a thing which
God hath made subjecting it to laws; but it
is an expression of the thought, the feeling,
the heart of God Himself.

The faces of some flowers lead me back to
the heart of God, and as His child I
hope I feel, in my lowly degree, what He
felt when, brooding over them, He said,
"They are good;"
that is,
"They are what I mean."

George MacDonald

A Rose in Winter

And so it goes
My January rose
Decidedly froze
In the snow
While chill winds blow
Alas, 'tis so
No bloom to grow?
No blossom to show?
My hope brought low
Yea—but though
In God I know
He is not slow
For redemption to bring
Ah! Soon the spring . . .

My poor February rose
Tragically in the throes
Of decay.
Dying 'ere it goes
Farewell.

A hold-out from last season
Braving winter for spring teasin'
If come to bloom 'twould be pleasin'

But, alas!

In March—I shed a tear
Behold, cometh the pruning shear
Cut back the refuse of last year
Make way—
A new rose destined to bloom here!

Ponder This: The rosebud was resilient. It persisted, taking a stubborn stand at the end of a thorny stem. The chill of October turned to November. Brown, brittle leaves blanketed the ground beneath it like a carpet. It was unmoved, bright pink, and supple still in December, though folded tight, unwilling to open to its full potential as the year closed. So birthed my musings on a January rose.

Hope deferred makes the heart sick,

but a dream fulfilled is a tree of life.

Proverbs 13:12 NLT

 I remained hopeful that, by some miracle, my rosebud would make it through winter and be the first bloom of spring. Yet, true to my poem, it decayed on its stem and was cut back in April. Even so, in due season, another replaced it. My hope was deferred—but not ultimately deterred. Think of a time in your life when you had hope of a miracle or an answer to prayer working out for you in a specific way. In the end, though, the Lord brought about very different circumstances. Did you feel the sickness of a hope deferred? Did you recognize when, in due season, your dream was fulfilled, but in a new and unexpected way? What did you learn of God in that time? What did you learn of yourself? Can God be trusted in every season?

My rosebud hung onto something that might be a testament to an impressive display of resilience or pure blind-to-truth stubbornness. Discerning the season to hold fast to a thing or lay down and relinquish a dream for pruning is a mark of both faith and wisdom. In loss, God generously pours His mercies into our hearts with renewal. Write a prayer of praise thanking God for pruning in your life.

When doubts filled
my mind,
your comfort gave me
renewed hope
and cheer.

Psalm 94:19 NLT

Through the Crack

The sidewalk.
Hardened cement.
A mixture of sand and pebbles
Rough to the touch.
Lifeless and void
Winding a path
According to the whims
Of the men who place it there.

In the midst of the solid stone
A crack.
Through the crack
A flower.

Nurtured by a drop of water
And a slice of sunshine.
The heat that hardens cement
Compels the seed felled
To life.

Supple and green.
Rooted and stable.
Every petal a masterpiece.
Every leaf a song.
Pointing straight and tall
Towards the heavens
Towards the sun;
Not looking to the left
Not looking to the right.
Its eyes fixed
Alone
On the fire in the sky
That feeds it.
Flowing with life
Abundant and full
Focusing only
On the source

Of its beauty and purpose.

In the midst of a hard
Aimless cement void
A crack.
A window.
Perhaps
An open door
Through which life and blessing
Flow
By the grace of the sun
And the creative perfection
Of a sovereign God.

Lord,
When I am in the midst of the enemy's void
Guard my steps from the harshness
And my life from despair.
Open my eyes to see the cracks
That my heart may hope
My thirst be quenched
My limbs caressed in warmth
And light.

Focusing only on You
The Source
Of my beauty in spirit
And purpose in life.

*The flowers that sleep by night, open their gentle eyes
and turn them to the day. The light, creation's mind, was
everywhere, and all things owned its power.*

Charles Dickens

Ponder This: Life is hard. If it were easy we wouldn't need God. And He wants us to want Him. To need Him. To hope in Him and believe Him when Jesus tells us:

With men this is impossible,
but with God all things are possible.

Matthew 19:26 NKJV

Sometimes the Lord gives the seed of our faith only a little crack of hope. But that's really all we need when fed by Light and Living Water from Heaven. Life sprouts, pushing up and out from between the hard places, to blossom into the beauty of its potential.

Are there hard places in your life crowding you and covering you with their heavy stone layers? Thank God for a hot season. Celebrate when it is cold. For the combined trauma of hot and cold cracks cement—and therein rests the potential for rescue. Focus on what Light breaks through the fracture and watch faith cultivate. Trust that droplets of Living Water will fill the cavern crevice where you break for a season, nurturing you from sprout to flourish. You rise above the harsh reality that once imprisoned you. Coming to maturity, you accomplish your destiny. Stronger for it to overcome the impossible.

Why, sometimes I've believed as many as
six impossible things before breakfast.

Lewis Carroll
Through the Looking Glass, 1872

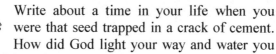 Write about a time in your life when you were that seed trapped in a crack of cement. How did God light your way and water you with provision so you could grow up and out, into your full potential? Write a Psalm reviewing the goodness of God to do the impossible for you in such a difficult season. Think of the trials of Israel throughout the Old Testament for further inspiration.

31

His Story

Part 1

Narrator:
In the beginning
God creates the heavens and the earth.
The heavens He fills
With abundant and powerful beings,
Angelic Ministers to the Almighty,
Guardians of His Will,
And a great Bandleader named, Lucifer,
Directing the glorious noise of Worship
Unto our Creator God.

But this commanding Archangel of Praise
Takes the adoration ordained for God alone
Upon himself,
And lifts his voice to proclaim
That he is God.

And there is war in heaven.

In his rebellion, he falls to the earth—
His beauty consumed by fire
Transformed to malevolent evil.

Chorus:
The Light, the Shine, the Beauty,
Of Creation to restore,
God Almighty Ruler
Always intended more.
No power can defeat Him
He reigns though darkness looms,
Because the everlasting love of God,
No evil can consume.

Narrator:
God divides this darkness
From His Light
And the Creator again creates.
Upon the earth He fashions
The land

33

The seas
The sun, moon, and stars
The growing things and living creatures
And
A Garden.

In this Garden
He shapes Man
Made in the image and likeness of God Himself
Male and Female
A Creature of thought and emotion
Of purpose and passion
And free will.
Designed to intimately know God
And to be known by Him
To love God and adore Him
Forever.

Creation enjoys a new Bandleader
Bringing continuous praise to God
Surpassing that of the Fallen Archangel
In the intimate zone of relationship—God and Man.

Chorus: The Light, the Shine, the Beauty
Of Creation to restore,
God Almighty Ruler
Always intended more.
No power can defeat Him
He reigns though darkness looms,
Because the everlasting love of God,
No evil can consume.

Narrator: Angry and destined for defeat,
Lucifer determines to pervert
The Light, the Shine, the Beauty
Of Created Man.
He plans to destroy Man's intimate relationship
With God
And make him a prisoner
Of his own sinful soul.

Man believes a lie—deceived.

By his own free will
He choses to reject God
And proclaims himself to be as God.

His spirit dies.

In his rebellion, all of Creation
Collapses
Under a curse.
Division. Schism.
The Light, the Shine, the Beauty of God
Must separate from His Beloved Creation,
Man.

Chorus: The Light, the Shine, the Beauty
Of Creation to restore.
God Almighty Ruler,
Always intended more.
No power can defeat Him,
He reigns though darkness looms,
Because the everlasting love of God
No evil can consume.

Narrator: But, God has a plan.
Only the Life of God
Can save the life of Man,
And restore their cherished love relationship
Ruptured.

He appoints a day and hour.

And in due season,
He calls
Michael.
The Archangel Warrior
Guardian of His Will,
Who cuts through the darkness
Thrusts aside the powers of Hell
Clears a cosmic highway

35

For God,
Himself
To step through the doors of eternity
Into the limitations of earthly time and space.

And through the body of a woman,
The seed of God's Spirit is born
Into the body of a Man.

The Way is made.
God is with Man.
God is Man.
The Man
Jesus Christ.

Chorus: The Light, the Shine, the Beauty
Of Creation to restore,
God Almighty Ruler
Always intended more.
No power can defeat Him,
He reigns though darkness looms,
Because the everlasting love of God,
No evil can consume.

To be continued . . .

Ponder This: I love history. This set me apart from my peers when I was in school. They thought it a dull chore reading about people and events from long ago. They didn't think the study of Western civilization had anything to do with them in the present. Why should they commit to memory a host of names and dates? How could the knowledge of such things prepare them for their future? It was a bore!

This is the unfortunate mindset I encountered during my classroom teaching days of middle and high school students. I resolved to change that. No one was bored in my history class because my emphasis was not on names and dates, but on the telling of an epic story. And, everyone loves a good story. Especially if it's filled with generous quantities of scandal, spectacle, and heroism. Noah Webster's definition of "history" in his *1828 Dictionary* concurs: *"What is the history of nations, but a narrative of the follies, crimes and miseries of man?"*

In truth, if you do not know where you came from—your history; you won't know who you are—your identity; and will have no firm direction for where you ought to go in the future. Our contemporary society sadly illustrates the effects of ignorance in historical truth, specifically His Story.

History is His Story
—the epic drama of God's ongoing relationship with His rebellious creation.

 His Story is a love story. A child rebels against a Father resulting in estrangement and chaos. A Lover is spurned and sacrifices much to restore relationship. Forces of good and evil clash with swords spanning the ages. A Hero is necessary to set things right. Each generation adds a chapter to the tale. Journal This: Do you love history? His Story? What part do you play in this epic love story?

Wings

My love has wings and we fly away,
And sit and sing
Throughout the day.
Sharing our love and joys and sorrows,
To keep forever, today, tomorrow.

My love has wings and up we fly,
Above the earth,
Above the sky.
To sit and wait upon a star,
Our eyes a'gazing out afar.
To distant lands of glee and sorrow,
To keep forever, today, tomorrow.

My love has wings and so we land,
Upon the earth,
Upon the sand.
And weep for those away off far,
Who once we saw from on a star.
Weep for those who cannot sing,
Because their love hasn't wings.

To share their sadness, woes, and sorrows.
To keep forever, today, tomorrow.

Ponder This: I wrote this poem at the age of fourteen in the mid-1970's. It reflects the idealism of youthful romantic thoughts, so dear to the heart of a young girl.

Reading these words today, I smile at the dramatic scene painted here—the sorrowful world the lovers see and the compassion they share for it in the midst of their personal joy and freedom.

I did not know the Lord at the time I wrote it, but He knew me. He had already called me, though it would be another ten years before I would respond to His call. Even still, isn't it interesting to read words poured forth from a naïve heart, expressing a secret elusive to my conscious at the time:

My true love is the Lord.
He has wings and gathers me in His arms,
Swept upwards we look upon a world larger than myself.
Our hearts become one—I rejoice with Him.
And mourn with Him.

The Lord's love and compassion for *"those who cannot sing, because their love hasn't wings,"* and our sharing together the burden of their *"sadness, woes, and sorrows,"* is an accurate picture of the longing in God's heart for the sinful, fallen race of man in need of salvation. This is the passion and purpose of God's heart. He shares this with those who love Him. The heart of God becomes the heart of man, *"to keep forever, today, tomorrow."*

 Even when I did not know Him, He loved me and inspired my art. All things are Christ's.

And why have I called you for this work?
Why did I call you by name when you did not know me?
                                          Isaiah 45:4 NLT

Isaiah 45 recalls Cyrus who did not know the Lord, yet was called by Him to accomplish a great task—presiding as King over the release and restoration of Israel as they were delivered out of Babylonian captivity. Think about a time in your life when the Lord showed His love for you though you did not know Him. How did He use you to accomplish His will? Did you sense His Presence then—or realize He'd been with you all along after you'd come into relationship with Him?

 Ponder This:

The Lord gave me this message:
"I knew you before I formed you in your mother's womb. Before you were born I set you apart and appointed you as my prophet to the nations."

"O Sovereign Lord," I said, "I can't speak for you! I'm too young!"

The Lord replied, "Don't say, 'I'm too young,' for you must go wherever I send you and say whatever I tell you. And don't be afraid of the people, for I will be with you and will protect you. I, the Lord, have spoken!" Then the Lord reached out and touched my mouth and said, "Look, I have put my words in your mouth!"

Jeremiah 1:4-9 NLT

Has the Lord called you? Has He put words in your mouth? Write about the passion and purposes of His heart that are the passion and purposes of your heart.

Rose Petal Rain

The bloom fades
Falls away
Rose petal rain

Beauty in the mud
Crushed beneath
The feet of
A beast
Deflowered

Leaving thorns in his wake
A foolish mistake
Selfish sin

Innocence lost
Too great a cost
Her feminine
Dignity
A princess
Dethroned
Turned to stone

Weather-beaten
Scarred

Redemption!
Cries she

Repentance.
Says He

Spring is
Her choice
Alone
To bloom again
Re-throned
Wiser

Ponder This: Have you known the pain of being "de-flowered?" It's not the same as the pruning shears taken to the rosebud, stubborn and frozen, in a season meant for dying. A violence has been perpetrated against the rose in this poem. A "beast" has stolen something precious, at its peak of potential.

Perhaps this poem speaks of the deception and destructive nature of sexual sin. But, the metaphor doesn't need to end there. Beasts of all shapes and sizes taunt and tear away at us on many fronts, seeking to steal, kill, and destroy our fragrant beauty in bloom:

- ❖ Divorce
- ❖ Prodigal children
- ❖ Debilitating illness
- ❖ Loss of income
- ❖ Fractured friendships
- ❖ Global wars
- ❖ Loss of personal freedom
- ❖ Overwhelming cares of this world

How many more can you list?

Though these trials crush our spirits and muddy our souls, the Lord is swift to save should we turn to Him with our cries for redemption. We repent of sin, doubt, and faithlessness. We choose the redraft of His Story in our life. He turns a beastly de-flowering into a blessed encounter with God's Grace and Mercy. He re-writes our story—from rebellion to royalty. Spring comes in due season, and buds blossom anew, re-throned.

 Journal This: Is there a chapter in your life where you need to cry "Redemption?" Journal your thoughts as prayer.

Retreat. Repent.
Redeem. Renew. Restore.

The Lord is close to the brokenhearted;
he rescues those whose spirits
are crushed.

Psalm 34:18 NLT

He heals the brokenhearted
and bandages their wounds.

Psalm 147:3 NLT

For this is how God loved the world: He
gave His one and only Son, so that
everyone who believes in Him will not
perish but have eternal life.

John 3:16 NLT

But if we confess our sins to him, he is
faithful and just to forgive us our sins and to
cleanse us from all wickedness.

1 John 1:9 NLT

Letter to a Hopeless Romantic

I lost my love within a dream,
    I woke and he was gone.
A fantasy? It didn't seem,
    'Tween midnight and the dawn.

He sang to me sweet melodies,
    Of love and hope and valor.
So brave, so kind, but where is he?
    Gone! Gone like a wilted flower.

I pressed a rose within a book,
    Though yellowed and crumpled with age.
Preserved for time, just a memory,
    He lies pressed upon this page.

What a fool of fools I was to dream,
    Of a love that could not be.
Hoping and wishing but knowing deep down,
    In his heart was no love for me.

Close your eyes and dream again,
    Dream he loves you, too.
Through false and fiction fairy tales
    He'll always love you true.

Rise and weep for slowly he fades,
    Goodbye my love begotten.
Goodbye sweet dreams and memories,
    Never to be forgotten.

Dear Estella,

    Thirty years ago I wrote this poem. Thirty years ago I was sixteen—like you are today. Thirty years ago I spent my days striving after a love with no future. Was I really in love—or just in love with being in love?

    Ah, the drama!

One day, the "he" I had so longed for was finally mine. A close friendship, fueled by dysfunctional dependency, became the romance I craved. For a few lovely moments, my dreams had come true. Then, I woke. I realized I wasn't quite as satisfied as I thought I should be. The rose, pressed between the pages of a book, turned to dust, discarded on a lonely shelf.

I was a captive of the tyrant "Ideal Romance." No matter where I turned I met prison walls. Nothing quenched me. Parasites within ate my joy. Melancholy rooted itself as my sole companion. Panic alarmed me in unexpected moments. Fear consumed me. Emptiness embraced me. Depression moved in.

Things weren't working out to fit my dreams— dreams that changed as swiftly as the second hand on the clock ticks to the next position.

Blinded by self-centeredness, I gave nothing to home and family. School morphed into a war zone laced with landmines; snipers hid in lockers and classrooms. I'd never be pretty enough, shapely enough, smart enough; wear the right clothes, say the right things. Guilty! Sentenced, by a jury of my adolescent peers. Decades later, their opinions, their judgments—are faded to obscurity. Passé with the passage of time.

Why think of my future? I'd out-grown the past. The present—a penitentiary. Help! My life is an asteroid hurling through space at dizzying speeds! Out of control! No direction! Destined for failure!

Where's a fairy godmother when you need your Prince Charming? Where's Superman when you need to be swept up in strong arms, safe and secure?

Truth is, Superman puts his blue spandex on one leg at a time just like everybody else. The dream fades in the raw light of imperfect reality. Do I have the wisdom to accept this?

Thirty years ago, I wrote this poem—a lonely, depressed young girl. Obsessed. Thinking my only salvation in life was to be attached to my "romantic ideal" through whom I'd find a valid reason to exist. I tried to shape the guy I wrote this poem about into that mold. No go.

Eventually, I did meet Superman. I tried to shape him into that mold, too. And, after my dream came true . . . that crashed. A no go, too.

So, there I was. Incarcerated in a jail cell I formed with my own hands. Stuck. Who could possibly rescue me and free me from this penal nightmare?

One day, from sheer exhaustion,
I died in my dungeon.

Funny thing about dying. When you do, there's nothing to hold you in anymore. Suddenly, absolutely nothing matters. You're not hungry. You don't worry about clothes or make-up. You could care less about keeping up with the popular trendsetters. You begin to see things from a new perspective. Instead of looking inward, you begin to look outward and upward and see:

For the Lord your God is living among you.
He is a mighty savior.
He will take delight in you with gladness.
He'll catch me up and twirl me about joyfully!

With his love, he will calm all your fears.
He'll hold me tenderly and caress my face as He
stares lovingly into my eyes—me—
the sole occupation of His adoring love!

He will rejoice over you with joyful songs.
Touching the depths of human passion, the music
and lyric of His love will thrill me to my recesses.
My Hero! My Lover! My Jesus!

Zephaniah 3:17 NLT

To you, my kindred spirit and hopeless romantic who hungers for this highest of ideals, I said all that to say this: Pursue your romance and destiny in the arms of the Prince of Peace. Let Him consume your fanciful dreams with the perfection and reality of His true love.

In His time, dear Estella, according to His purposes, He will send you your earthly Prince Charming. *And, they all lived happily ever after . . .*

Love, Miss Kathy

 My poor little friend! How well I knew her heart. Her lamentations mirrored my own when I was her age. I didn't know the Lord as my Savior and Lover back then. I lacked true wisdom to fight the worldly temptations trying to divert my path to places God had not called me. Life experience taught me the lessons I shared with her. She had walked with the Lord since childhood, yet battled beasts seeking to de-flower her of royal standing.

In hindsight, I am thankful for the battles of my youth. God prepared me to speak into the lives of young women in the generation to follow. Forgiveness heals the past and makes it a useful tool for the present, informing my future to the Glory of God.

Write about these truths in your life. Are you the wise and weathered woman teaching the younger, or are you, like Estella, fighting beasts, looking for a Hero to save the day? Who is your Superman? What must you do to fortify yourself in the fight, Princess?

Don't copy the behavior and customs of this
world, but let God transform you into a
new person by changing the way you think.
Then you will learn to know God's will for
you, which is good and pleasing
and perfect.

Romans 12:2 NLT

Whatever things are true, whatever things
are noble, whatever things are just,
whatever things are pure, whatever things
are lovely, whatever things are of good
report, if there is any virtue and if there is
anything praiseworthy —
meditate on these things.

Philippians 4:8 NKJV

Knights in Shining Armor
And Other Heroes I Have Known

Knights in shining armor
And other heroes I have known,
Are merely a reflection
Of the glories of Your throne.

A Trinity of facets;
O, Your height! Your width! Your depth!
Unmatched in all Your grandeur
How you take away my breath!

Mankind can scarce but mirror
All Your splendor in small measure;
A meager penny version,
Not the full weight of Your treasure.

Why then, when cruel beasts roar
And their tanks roll into town,
Do I find that rather than gaze up,
My countenance turns down.

I seek a worldly refuge,
I seek a person to call, Lord;
Positioned as a steadfast shield,
Who wields a mighty sword.

I pursue mere man to save me
Wondering why one can't be found.
No wonder Unrest captures me,
With saviors so earthbound.

Knights in shining armor
And other heroes I have known,
Have yet to rescue damsels
Duly tossed and tempest blown.

But, my God, You are so worthy!
But, my King, You are so strong!
You sweep me off my feet, Sweet Lord!
I thrill in Rapture's song!

Knights in shining armor
And other heroes I have known,
Serve but to stir desire
That when followed lead me home.

Home! Home, the place of refuge
Held fast by His strong arm.
Embraced in Love—in shielded bliss,
Is where I'm safe from harm.

Ponder This: Here's a poem full of romantic imagery. Have you ever thought of your relationship with God in these terms? The idea that we are "damsels in distress" requiring a hero to swoop in and save the day is largely panned in popular culture. These days, with all the contrived confusion tilting the battle of the sexes into overdrive, harboring such romantic desires is considered weak, if not foolish.

But the Lord uses the foolish things to confound the wise (1 Corinthians 1:18-25). I prefer to be of use to the Lord so I'm good with that. Being foolish. And hopelessly in love with my King and my God.

The shield of His Body and Blood are only matched by the Sword of His Word, wielded with cosmic power to raise the dead to life—the very thing this damsel in distress needs for deliverance.

Jesus is my Knight in Shining Armor!

ROMANCE *n.*

A fabulous relation or story of adventures and incidents; a tale of extraordinary adventures, fictitious and often extravagant, usually a tale of love or war, subjects interesting the sensibilities of the heart, or the passions of wonder and curiosity.

Webster's 1828 Dictionary

 The Bible is filled with romance: *"tales of extraordinary adventures . . . love or war, subjects interesting the sensibilities of the heart, or the passions of wonder and curiosity."*

Many of literature's greatest romances date to the times of medieval chivalry where exploits by knights in shining armor is the norm. Noble quests, heroic deeds, and tragic sacrifices stir hearts and passions. Such tales feed the hunger of men and women seeking rescue from the evils in a sinful world. It is a commonplace most people share—the desire for love to conquer all. Isn't that God's story—His Story—told in the Living Word of Jesus Christ? Reflectively read the *Song of Solomon* in the Bible. Write your thoughts on it in relation to the *Knights in Shining Armor* poem, and the quote below from my play *Intimate Zones*:

> God's really quite a romantic fellow, you know. So lavish and dashing in appearance. He strolls about Creation dressed in flash and brilliance as the sunset. He wears a magnificent cape draped about Him as a verdant valley slope. His fragrance is as a sumptuous meadow, scented by thousands of wildflowers and musk. His features are etched strong—fixed as the mountain peaks. He is faithful as the sea and the tick-tock of time. His arms ever surround me as the atmosphere embraces the earth. Oh! How I love You, my Lord! My Life!
>
> Monologue excerpt of Unspeakable Joy

His Story

Part 2

Narrator: God is with Man.
God is Man.
The Man
Jesus Christ.

Chorus: The Light, the Shine, the Beauty
Of Creation to restore,
God Almighty Ruler
Always intended more.
No power can defeat Him
He reigns though darkness looms
Because the everlasting love of God,
No evil can consume.

Narrator: A Divine battle strategy
Takes center stage.
The intimacy between the Creator
And His created Man
Will be forever restored;
The effect of Lucifer's rebellion on the earth—
Destroyed.

Chorus: Look into His eyes
Jesus the Man.
The passion in His gaze.
The tenderness of His touch.
A Divine Romance
Captivates your soul
You are changed.

Call to Him—He hears.
There's power in His Name.
Healer of the wounded.
Broken hearts made new.
Walk Hand in hand
As in the Beginning

57

You are changed.

Listen to His Voice
Living Word of Wisdom,
The Substance of Truth.
Life to Man's heart,
Words of simplicity,
Tangible relevancy,
You are changed.

Narrator: He participates in the grand adventure
Of living!
Laughing. Crying. Playing.
Growing weary.
Knowing hunger.
Dancing for joy.
Frustrated in anger.
Loved. Hated. Misunderstood.
Tempted in all things common to Man.
Sympathetic with the complexities of the soul.
Yet—God.
Pure. Sinless. Perfection.

Thirty-three years a generation of Mankind
Knew the privilege of God in the Flesh.
Appearing Live and In Person!
On a whirlwind World Tour.
Demonstrating Life
As He designed it to be lived.
Till the critical execution of
The Plan.
His Victorious Plan!
The final engagement at
Lucifer's Coliseum.

Chorus: Look into His eyes
Jesus the Man.
Scorned. Rejected.
Condemned to die.
With passion in His gaze

Forgiveness on His Lips,
He bought Man's pain,
Man's sin,
Man's death,
Paying cash with His Life.
Are you changed?

Narrator: Oh Man! Why do you mourn so?
Dear Soul! Why do you cry?
Don't you know
Your God's not dead—
He's Alive!

Chorus: The Light, the Shine, the Beauty
Of Creation He restored.
Jesus! Mighty! Ruler!
Always intended more.
Death could not defeat Him.
He walked right out of that tomb—
Because the everlasting love of God
No sin can consume!

Protagonist Response:
I'm ready to hear about Jesus the Man
Jesus the God
Who loved me just where I am.
Ready to Believe—Truth!
I am nothing without Him.
He died for me.
He died for me!
I am changed.

Chorus: The Light, the Shine, the Beauty
Of Creation He restored.
Jesus! Mighty! Ruler!
Always intended more.
Death could not defeat Him.
He walked right out of that tomb!
Because the everlasting love of God
No sin can consume!

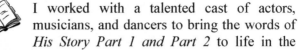 I worked with a talented cast of actors, musicians, and dancers to bring the words of *His Story Part 1 and Part 2* to life in the context of a longer stage play. We understood our efforts were insignificant apart from the anointing of the Holy Spirit. We were changed through His Story as story.

Can you empathize with the heart of God yearning to restore His Beloved to Himself? Are you pierced to the depths to consider the great price paid for YOU? Pour out your thoughts through your pen to your journal. Allow yourself to burrow down into the full impact of His Story in your life—every facet of your life. How are you changed?

 Be a playwright. Choose a story from His Story and break it down into scenes. How would you assign parts and lines? How would you direct the action? If you were filming it, how would you zoom in on the close-ups to capture the full impact of each character's expressiveness?

 Use the two Scriptures on the facing page, Romans 5:8 and Romans 10:9, to write lyrics to a song illustrating their truths. You are composing a Psalm—much like His Story. Make it personal to your experience in learning to be:

. . . ready to hear about Jesus the Man
Jesus the God
Who loved me just where I am.
Ready to Believe—Truth!
I am nothing without Him.
He died for me.
He died for me!
I am changed.

*But God demonstrates His own love toward
us, in that while we were still sinners,
Christ died for us.*

Romans 5:8 NLT

*If you confess with your mouth the Lord Jesus
and believe in your heart that God has raised
Him from the dead, you will be saved.*

Romans 10:9 NLT

...azing. I went
...We drove to the
...ate brunch, we
...snorkling for couple
...to go to the nearby
...walked up the hill
...e saw an amazing view
...s clear and not so
...d after a long walk
...on how and came back
...d a hotel for 2 nights.
...he night street market
...stuffs for our family
...hold around so on.

Exhausted but really fun. None of us took a shower
that night! omg. Tomorrow we will start a
journey again !!

TTYL Diary ☺

Journal:
Genesis of a Writer's Reverie

My daughter is very creative. As a child she loved to draw pictures and write poems passionately portraying her undying love for Mommy and Daddy.

One day, she drew a picture of me as a queen. I taped it to our refrigerator. Then there was the day she drew a picture of me with lots of hearts around my head, proclaiming her affections—and my beauty—even in the light of the monster zit I'd battled on my face that week. As a matter of fact, she captured the nasty blemish in her drawing of me. I taped that on the refrigerator too—careful to make sure a decorative magnet securely covered the offending mark.

My husband and I were blessed weekly with Bethany's love notes in all their artistic splendor. We cherished every one and I kept a little file to store them for future reference, when I might chance to be a tad unpopular in declaring a disappointing parental edict. A few of these paper canvases I've glued into my journals—a place of higher honor. How I loved to receive her little masterpieces, creatively designed and dedicated to the love of—Mom.

God really loves that, too.

He really loves it when His creative children use their creative gifts to design and dedicate artistic expressions—the works of their hands—to glorify Him. As His little children, our life should be a work of art expressing who He is as Father God, what He has done for us as divine Savior, and how grateful we are to intimately know Him as our loving Lord. The creative, artistic, dramatic arts become a true masterpiece when used in liberty of expression and excellence of skill to worship the Creative God from whom they were inherited.

When Jesus walked the very earth He had formed, all Creation was subject to His commands: fish crowded into nets (John 21:4-6), stormy seas becalmed (Matthew 8:23-27), figs withered on the tree (Matthew 21:18-19). All Creation knew when their Creator touched the earth and strolled about His fragrant fields.

During His triumphal entry into Jerusalem, had the multitudes and disciples not praised God, *". . . with a loud voice for all the mighty works they had seen,"* Jesus knew, *". . . if these should keep silent, the very rocks would immediately cry out."* (Luke 19:37-40 NKJV)

Rocks talk? You bet!

They intimately knew the fingers, deft and sure, that carved them into the landscape. They were a part of a total body of work created by a Master Artist who sculpted, painted, scripted, and spoke: beauty, purpose, value, and meaning into every detail of His Masterpiece with symbolic vocabulary. This symbolic vocabulary is a universal language through which God reveals Himself so that all men from all cultures at all times are able to discern Him. This is why Romans 1:20 NKJV warns us:

"For since the creation of the world His invisible attributes are clearly seen, being understood by the things that are made, even His eternal power and God-head, so that they [all mankind] are without excuse."

My most intimate moments with the Lord happen when I'm doing something creative, beginning with stillness and a thoughtful reverie.

Whether it's writing, performing, or crafting a work of visual mixed-media art, I sense His inspiration surge through me as my little creation becomes, in a sense, a passionate love letter to my Lord. Apart from Him, I can do nothing.

And, 'ere you despair believing yourself to not be creative—you do error. Our talents may vary, as do our callings, but we are possessed of so many gifts, all of which we are to use creatively. The mother, homemaker, caretaker, house cleaner, office secretary, retail clerk, business owner, executive manager, and blogger alike, are blessed with creative gifts the Lord desires to develop in each.

Whatever constitutes your life, He molds as a Masterpiece to His purposes in the earth. Or in the home, family, church, and community at large—if you will allow Him to so woo you.

I find inspiration for the works of my hands during contemplative times of prayer and quiet worship. Sometimes it is inspiration for ministry service to another. Daily, it is direction in my creative call as a writer—a thought becomes a line of verse, which becomes a story idea, or character. When I obediently follow through and put pen to paper, creative expression bubbles forth. Something of God is birthed, but it is yet to be perfected. That will require more work.

More of the Master's work in me.

I wrote one such story in a feeble attempt to describe what it felt like to love God, and be loved by Him. I was learning how His love transforms my life into a true Masterpiece—reflecting His goodness and glory. But, it doesn't happen swiftly.

The Master Artist takes his time, shepherding every inch of the canvas of my life with just the right color, line, and perspective; using just the right brush to the task—patiently allowing each layer of imagery to dry in place before returning with the next stroke.

And, the next.

He alone decides the details of background, foreground, and overall composition. In the landscape meadows of a canvas, He meets me. Daily. In the idyllic sanctuary of the soul and spirit, I meet Him. Seeking completion. A writer's reverie. Face to face with the Master; the Shepherd of my soul—the Suitor of my heart.

Metaphorical language, so often used in Scripture, is my favorite storytelling device. If asked to describe an aspect of my love relationship with God, I might pour out my words in prose, poetry, or prayer. As a playwright, I have composed countless theatrical dramas for the stage exploring the nuances of biblical truth through story.

Though human creativity has its boundaries, God's creativity in our lives does not. He is constantly inspiring our spirits to draw close to Him to receive more of Him. To be changed. Transformed. Fashioned for Him, into His Masterpiece.

How ought we respond to such Artistry?

The supreme duty of the creature

for time and eternity

is to worship the Creator.

my own heart has been

relentlessly pursued

by the Lion of Worship . . .

stalked by worship's

awesome and majestic

reality . . .

LarMar Boshman

Like an apple tree among the
trees of the woods, so is my
Beloved among the sons,
I sat down in His shade with
great delight and His fruit was
sweet to my taste.
Song of Solomon 2:3 NLT

Masterpiece in the Meadow

Joyful Heart stirs as early morning sunrays filter through the sheltering tree limbs above, painting a dappling of light patterns about her woolly white coat. Turning her head towards the gentle warmth of the light, a contented smile spreads across her face as she blinks her eyes open.

What a lovely new day! A fresh scent of wildflower wafts by and she jumps to her feet to readily grab hold of it. How she loves the sweet aromas of her beloved Meadow.

Before, when she lived in the valley mud-bogs, sweet, lovely scents never drifted in the air. Everything bore the heavy odors of mold, mildew, and dung. She shakes her head remembering how foolish she was in those days, clinging to such refuse. But, she knew naught else at the time.

So, when the Suitor approached, inviting her to His Meadow, she declined to surrender her mud-bog and follow Him to His Fragrant Fields. What He described to her seemed unrealistic. Surely not for her. She tried to imagine the things He spoke of, but they didn't fit in her Experience Box.

"It's just not big enough to hold what You offer," she complained. "I can't believe it and don't see such things ever fitting into my Box."

"Perhaps," the Suitor gently countered, "you would be best served if I gave you a New Experience Box." For an instant, her heart skipped a beat at the soothing sound of His voice, and the kindness in his piercing eyes looking straight through her as he spoke. "I have a lovely Box in mind just for you. It's very large and has lots of space to hold many great and wonderful things. When you place it in My Sunlight, it sparkles and glows. Others see it from far off and draw near to look upon your great possession in awe. And, with desire."

Her momentary reverie at His inviting words abruptly broke. She clutched tight to her little Box pouting her lips. "If it is so awesome and desired," she contended, "then someone might steal it from me."

"Never!" asserted the Suitor. "Nobody needs to steal what I give free to all."

She was not convinced. "Well, no matter," she said, "my simple little Experience Box may not be so very awesome, but it is mine. *Mine!*"

This was true.

It was her own and she had had it for quite some time. It was comfortable and familiar. The thought of trading it in on something so spacious and unimaginable seemed too great a risk. A reckless request!

The Suitor left that day, sighing as He went. She grieved Him with her rejection. But to her, it was safer to wallow in the valley mud-bog Experience Box she knew, then venture into the unbelievable promise of a New Experience Box. A journey into the unknown required a substantial leap of faith. Growth into a greater thing meant leaving behind something. The very idea was too fearful to fit in her Box!

However, the Suitor, a persistent fellow not given to despair, arrived the following day—with a gift.

"What have You brought?" she queried, with tempered curiosity.

"These are for you." He said, extending a fistful of tiny violets and buttercups. "I searched My entire Meadow for something that might possibly fit into your Experience Box. I think these are sufficiently small. Perhaps, if you keep them for a while, you may like them enough to try to make room in your Box for other small items from My Meadow."

Her brow furrowed. She blinked her eyes in disbelief. Who was she that such a Suitor, so far above her in every way, should continue to address her in this manner? She knew of His Story. A love story filled with heroic exploits, marvels, and a sacrifice so great that songs where sung about Him from canyon to mountain peaks. Why was a Champion such as He standing before her, beckoning with violets and buttercups?

As though hearing her thoughts He said, "I am the Suitor. The Shepherd seeking sheep. If these became a familiar comfort to you, maybe then you'd let me give you a New Experience Box big enough to hold all the delights I could fill it with."

She remembers the moment she first requited His advance, and reached forward to take hold of His gift. She had never seen anything so beautiful! Her furrowed brow of trepidation softened with a serene sense of calm. Of peace. Carefully, she lay the tiny bouquet of wildflowers in her little Experience Box, filling it to overflowing

But, she didn't notice that, at first.

Captivated by a closer inspection, she froze, mesmerized at the unique perfection of every petal. She marveled how each color differed, brilliant with life! Her nostrils tingled with the fresh fragrance dancing about her head. The Suitor called it "sweet."

"If you come with Me to live in My Meadow," He invited, "not only will I give you a New Experience Box, but, I will make all things new. You will wear a perfume with a sweeter aroma than these wildflowers."

It was more than she could endure. He won her heart. She no longer questioned why He should pursue her with His love. It no longer seemed important that she be worthy to be loved. He was worthy to be loved by her. That alone mattered.

Inhaling deeply, Joyful Heart glances over to her New Experience Box the Suitor gave her that day. It contained the first bouquet of wildflowers, as well as many other beautiful gifts He'd lavished upon her. There were many sparkling jewels. Azure blue skies and shooting stars. Cleansing waterfalls and quiet shady groves. Soft beachy sands, and gray clouds of solitude and silver linings. Each gift, like the strokes of a master painter's brush, continues to color her world anew— creating and recreating her heart. A Masterpiece!

But, by far, her favorite gift is the perfume He promised her.

Once she followed Him, in all abandon, to the Meadow, she never again knew the heaviness of hard, dried clay from the valley mud-bog clinging to her coat. She shines now, woolly white and clean. Each day she reverently lifts her perfume atomizer from the Box and sprays herself all about with the sweet aroma.

Today is not to be different. With a spritz here, and a dab behind the ears there, the fragrance engulfs her, blending with the surrounding wildflower scents, swelling in chorus. Her playful giggle melts into hearty laughter as she kicks her heels, dancing about the expanse of the Meadow.

This is why the Suitor calls her Joyful Heart. Her New Experience Box brims with Rejoicing and often overflows with Passion. The Shepherd can smell her fragrance from any point in His vast Meadow. He immediately runs to her side at the scent of it. He loves the liberality with which she bathes in her perfume. It blesses Him so, to frolic about with Joyful Heart, taking pleasure in her presence. One might be hard pressed to state which of the two receives the greater blessing.

When caught up in the Meadow of the Suitor, time passes unnoticed. Perhaps it is hours—maybe even days—before the jubilant laughter and dancing, with shouts of joy, subsides into a quiet embrace. She stands, swaying in the fresh breeze, then collapses in ecstasy, kneeling at the feet of her Beloved Shepherd—the Suitor of her soul.

In quiet communion.
In expressive silence.
She is at peace in his Presence.
A Masterpiece in the Meadow.
Mud-bogs and mildew are eons away.
Her whole desire is to spend eternity
exactly where she is—

Living life as a fragrant,

sweet-smelling aroma,

pleasing to her Lord.

Ponder This: Story has a way of sifting through the layers of self, to the heart, where truth hides. Joyful Heart allows the Suitor to woo her truths to the surface, where they are improved upon with Christ-centered insight, exchanged for *His* Truth entirely. The transformed life is a Masterpiece:

And so, dear brothers and sisters,
I plead with you to give your bodies to God
because of all he has done for you.
Let them be a living and holy sacrifice
—the kind he will find acceptable.
This is truly the way to worship him.
Don't copy the behavior and customs of this world,
but let God transform you into a new person
by changing the way you think.
Then you will learn to know God's will for you,
which is good and pleasing and perfect.
Romans 12:1-2 NLT

 What were the things you kept in your mud-bog Experience Box before Jesus wooed your heart to Himself?

 What was the "small" gift He gave you that first captivated your spirit the way Joyful Heart was captivated by that first tiny bouquet of wildflowers?

 Consider the gifts Joyful Heart kept in her New Experience Box:

❖ Sparkling jewels
❖ Azure blue skies
❖ Shooting stars
❖ Cleansing waterfalls
❖ Quiet shady groves
❖ Soft beachy sands
❖ Gray clouds of solitude and silver linings
❖ Fragrant perfume

Choose at least three of them to metaphorically compare to a gift God has given you in your life. Describe the gift and how He has used it to make you into His Masterpiece. Suppose a card came with each gift. What Scripture would He write on the card attached to that gift and why?

 As you meditate on these things and how God's Word relates to His work in your life, take some time to liberally spritz yourself with the "perfume of praise" as a fragrant, sweet smelling aroma, pleasing to your Lord. Take time to live today with a Joyful Heart—cloistered with the Lover of your soul. Journal this—what does praise look like in practical terms?

Journal:
The Efficacy of Retreat

I am a writer. I write. Everyday. One thing or another. Lately, it's been hours in one position in front of my laptop working on a plethora of projects and publishing deadlines. I stare at my Focus List into which I must pour my energies.

I love to write. But, I'm exhausted!

Making daily time for reflection and journaling in the midst of the work-clutter on my drawing board, is beyond difficult. What's a lover of God, writing and journaling to do?

In times past, I've forced myself into a place of retreat. Retreat—to advance.

A good example of that is when I taught at a school in Chesapeake, Virginia during the mid-1990's. I taught drama and wrote original plays for production in addition to promotional work for the school in general. My plate was full with a robust year of events and activities, plus the raising of my own two elementary aged children. Time for personal reading, reflection, and journaling, curled up in a thoughtful position on an overstuffed chair with a cuppa tea, was not easily worked into my routine.

Retreat days must be scheduled in order to meet the Lord with a journal and a generous time allotment. To that end, a most memorable retreat day was planned with a young student photographer from the school. He knew I was fascinated with the ruins of an abandoned dairy farm I passed on the way to work each day. Such a setting held the same allurements for me as the ancient stone ruins dotting the landscapes of England, Scotland,

and Ireland—romantic memorials of castles and monasteries, once teeming with life and purpose. Would I find the same in these ruins?

The collection of empty barns, stalls, and sheds, in various states of decay and overgrowth, enthralled my friend's artistic spirit, too. He planned to photograph them one Saturday morning and invited me along to explore with him. I was happy for the invite for I'd have never ventured to such a desolate place alone. There was no telling what might be discovered there.

Securing childcare for the morning, I met him on the grounds with a fold-out chair, snack food, sketch pad, journal, Bible, and writing instruments. While he wandered about clicking away with his fancy camera and lenses, I found my quiet place under a shade tree in front of a deliciously deteriorating ancient barn.

I drank in the crumbling landscape before me— studying every weathered detail. I wrote what I saw in simple words and staccato phrases. I listened to the symphony-like sounds of nature surrounding me and attempted to record them with my pen.

Prayerfully, I listened for God's still, small voice to inspire my spirit with insight. I wondered at the significance—the purpose—of these ruins, and my retreat there. Reviewing the jumble of unrelated words I'd scribbled on the page, my sloppy, stumbling prose tightened into poetic free verse with a bit of editing. A love letter. Expressed, perhaps, as a drama played out on a stage. Five scenes sandwiched between a Prologue and Epilogue. The perfect literary vehicle for a romance. In the ruins.

I went up on the hill

and walked about

until twilight had deepened

into an autumn night

with a benediction

of starry quietude over it.

I was alone but not lonely.

I was a queen in halls of fancy.

Lucy Maud Montgomery
"Emily's Quest"

The Romance in the Ruins

Prologue:

There's an abandoned dairy farm
Near my home.
I drive past it every day.
Each time I do
It beckons me.

A clump of forgotten barns.
        Rotting away.
                In overgrown brush.
Each time I pass them
I sense the ambiance of—
Romance.
A story to tell.
        A moment of rest.
                A call to come.
Come.
To the Romance in the Ruins.

Scene 1:

I longed for the day
I could just get away
To a place
        Peaceful.
                Serene.
Perhaps forgotten.
        To think.
                To dream.

What would I hear?
What secrets discover?
The romance in the ruins!
A rendezvous
With a Lover.

He'll speak in the breeze
He'll laugh
        Joyous in song
Throated through sparrows

Cooed softly by pigeons
Who roost amid
The tattered framework
    Of a sheltered place
        Long abandoned.
The romance in the ruins
    Alive with silence.
        Peaceful.
            Serene.
I've not forgotten.

Scene 2:   Though it seems
    So long—
        So much—
Crowding my days.
    Drowning my song.
But now here I sit.
    Here I sing.
From my heart to my pen
    It flows
Across the lines on a page.
    Verse!
Minimal in rhyme.
    No sound.
Still the song is mine.

A symphony!
A response!
To the warm winds
    That toss my hair
        And caress my body.
And the sun,
    Shining.
        Twinkling through
            Teasing clouds.
And the color of day,
    Peaceful.
        Serene.
Ahhhh . . . Rest.
The romance in the ruins.

Scene 3:   I remember a place like this
                                From my youth
                        When days were slower
                                And simpler.
                        It was called
                                The Field.
                        But first—
                        I must trek through the Great Woods
                        On a path hewn
                        From motorcycle wheels.
                        But I imagine it
                                Hewn by other
                                        Pilgrims.
                                                Searching, too.

                        And under the menacing
                                Dense foliage
                                        I shiver.
                        Tales of the ghastly!
                        A bloody hand
                                Follows me.
                                        Stalking.
                        A morbid imagination—
                        A frightful sensation—
                        Who will save me?

                        I expect . . .
                                HIM!
                        From behind any tree—
                                Grand and gallant.
                                        Looking for me.
                                                Only.

                        The horrors cut asunder
                        I'm swept off my feet—
                        We gallop through
                                To the end of the trail
                                        To the Field.
                        Broad in expanse
                                Lush and lovely.

Which direction do we run in first?
Can we fly?
Yes . . . please!

The Freedom!
    The Enchantment!
        Peaceful.
            Serene.
Ahhhh . . . the Rest.

Scene 4:   These ruins know Rest
Alone—
    But not lonely.
Often forgotten
    But glad.

Broken brickwork.
    Shattered glass.
        Faded boards
            Creaking.
A secluded dumping ground
There's a freezer upside-down.
And a washing machine.
Something made of fiberglass
    I don't know what.

And above it all
    Poetic barns still loom.
See the stables
    Abundant still
        With feed straw
And the milking stations.
    The pastures beyond.
Life flowed here!
A bustle of activity
Voices eager and anxious
    For the day's work.
Now all is quiet.
    Peaceful.
        Serene.

Ahhhh . . . the romance in the ruins
Yet speaks!

Scene 5:   There is Life here!
The secrets I discover
A rendezvous
            With my Lover.

He brings a gift
            More precious than gold
                        To me.
It's Free.

In the quiet
            I hear Him sing
                        A lullaby.
Here is Peace.
            Ahhhh . . . the Rest.

His Rest.

And through the cricket's violin
            And the reeds of the trees;
Through the lyric of the birds
            And the splash of blue sky;
Through that red barn door
Hanging askew
            So like me
Guarding the loft
            And the creeping vines
Branches and limbs
Interlocked.
Even in the debris
            Of modern living
                        Scattered carelessly
Here . . . There

In all He speaks!
            Peace.
                        Serenity.

Rest.

Alone.
        But not lonely.
Tucked away.
        Forgotten.
           And glad.

Scene 6:   It is a glorious gift My Lover gives.
He knows me well.
Swept off my feet
        These ruins
           A field of pleasure.
Which direction do I run in first?
I don't know
But I'm free to fly!
Shall we dance a galliard
        Before we waltz?
No matter to me
        So long as
           My Lover leads.

Epilogue: There's an abandoned dairy farm
Near my home.
A place that once produced nourishment
For the body
        Nourishes now my soul.
           And therein I find Life!
           For the spirit.

Whenever I stroll through an antique shop I do so with my companions, Awe and Wonder. Things. Old things. Old things marred from use—or abuse. Old things past their prime of purpose. Old things—which once were new. Coveted. Celebrated. Now, cast away to decay. Ruins. Ruined.

You know what I do with stuff like that? I decorate with it. Repurpose it. I fill my house with worn and weathered this and thats from bygone times. I'm at home among them and the stories they tell. Perhaps it's a romance. Or a fantastic tale of legend and adventure with joyful peaks, and valleys of gloom, and in Christ— a happily ever after, of course.

It's not a new tale told. There's nothing new under the sun. Old or new stories call me to come away to a place of discovery—the glory of His Story. Is there a precious ruin in your life? A trinket from your grandmother? A souvenir from your childhood? A treasure you picked up in a thrift shop? Write its story. Can you hear His Story in its story?

The ancient church built splendid cathedrals spanning magnificent heights, hewn from stone and marble. Master artists embedded His Story into the stone—chiseled through sculpture, painted as murals, woven as tapestries. Sunlight set colorful stained glass windows ablaze with depictions of His Word from Genesis to Revelations. Pilgrims sought refuge in these glorious edifices for centuries.

Few remain standing intact today. Many are ruined shells of their former grandeur. Some are mere piles of stones clumped on a green landscape with only the wind for company. But, no matter their condition— the romance of their story remains in the ruins. Much like that abandoned dairy farm. Or my own soul in a forlorn season. Explore these thoughts in your journal.

Do you need to embrace your romance in His Story? Reread *The Romance in the Ruins* one section at a time. Relate the following Scriptures to each scene and write your thoughts.

Prologue

My heart has heard you say,
"Come and talk with me."
And my heart responds,
"Lord, I am coming."
Psalm 27:8 NLT

Scene 1

It is useless for you to work so hard from early morning
until late at night, anxiously working for food to eat;
for God gives rest to his loved ones.
Psalm 127:2 NLT

Before daybreak the next morning, Jesus got up and
went out to an isolated place to pray.
Mark 1:35 NLT

Scene 2

Then Jesus said, "Come to me, all of you who are weary
and carry heavy burdens, and I will give you rest. Take
my yoke upon you. Let me teach you, because I am
humble and gentle at heart, and you will find rest
for your souls.
Matthew 11:28-29 NLT

Scene 3

See, God has come to save me. I will trust in him and not
be afraid. The LORD GOD is my strength and my
song; he has given me victory.
Isaiah 12:2

Scene 4

For ever since the world was created,
people have seen the earth and sky.
Through everything God made,
they can clearly see his invisible qualities—
his eternal power and divine nature.
So they have no excuse for not knowing God.
Romans 1:20 NLT

Scene 5

My beloved spoke, and said to me:
"Rise up, my love, my fair one,
And come away.
For lo, the winter is past,
The rain is over and gone.
The flowers appear on the earth;
The time of singing has come,
And the voice of the turtledove
Is heard in our land.
Song of Solomon 2:10-12 NKJV

Scene 6

I have loved you with an everlasting love;
Therefore with lovingkindness I have drawn you.
Again I will build you, and you shall be rebuilt,
O virgin of Israel!
You shall again be adorned with your tambourines,
And shall go forth in the dances of those who rejoice.
Jeremiah 31:3-4 NKJV

He leads the humble in doing right,
teaching them his way.
The Lord leads with unfailing love and faithfulness
all who keep his covenant and obey his demands.
Psalm 25:9-10 NLT

About Pageant Wagons

In the beginning the Word already existed.
The Word was with God, and the Word was God.
The Word gave life to everything that was created,
and his life brought light to everyone.
The light shines in the darkness,
and the darkness can never extinguish it.

John 1:1-5 NLT

Once upon a time, after the libraries were burned and the villages sacked, and a great darkness covered Western Europe, the Pageant Wagons rolled into town. And—there was light.

True story.

It's a slice of history—His Story—not many people know about. They don't teach it in school anymore. However, it's true. It happened—and, it can happen again.

My passion for literacy and learning blossomed through my training in Principle Approach Education. This historic, classical, biblical methodology equips the teacher to master a subject as a "living textbook." The timeline of Providential history and primary sourced documents illustrate when and how each subject relates to God's story from Creation to today. Students are schooled to:

- ❖ Understand the tenants of the subject
- ❖ Discern its relation to biblical truth
- ❖ Identify its relation to their own lives
- ❖ Develop a biblical worldview

This philosophy of education was employed throughout the founding and early years of America. The primary textbook in home and school for over two hundred years was the Bible. Students were taught how to learn, think, and reason, within each discipline. Critical thought and productive industry enjoyed reward, forming the minds and hearts of the noble generation of patriots and leaders called by God to craft our national government. This exceptional, learned group of men and women, understood the lessons of history and unmatched value of, as Samuel Adams put it, "the Christian system." They created a Constitutional Republican form of human government based on the belief that a literate society grounded in the firm foundation of biblical principles and worldview is necessary to life, liberty and the pursuit of happiness. Their faith, vision, and sacrifice maintains a powerful global impact for the Gospel of Jesus Christ, today.

Yet, just five hundred years before the first explorers and colonists arrived on American shores, their ancestors in Western Europe were still navigating their way through the turbulence in their society, upended in the wake of the fall of Rome—five hundred years earlier in 410AD.

By that time, the Christian church was growing rapidly, even after centuries of horrific persecution. Roman society blanketed the world as far north as Britain. But, due to the pagan perversity of the culture and a succession of corrupt leaders, their spiral into decline and decay weakened them. Though an educated society in many respects, it was not a godly society. The imbalance made them vulnerable to attack.

So, when the Danube River froze in the winter of 410AD, illiterate hordes of barbarians from the north crossed the natural water border into the warmer climates of the wealthy southern portions of Europe. They set their sights on Rome, to take hold of the riches in these new territories. Cutting a violent swath through the geography of the region, whole towns and villages were pillaged, lives and fortunes lost, and Rome found itself unequal to stand against the tide. A military recall of all their regiments from every reach of their domain, in order to defend their capital, stripped Britain of her only protective forces. But, to no avail.

Rome was sacked. Ultimately, the civilized society in Europe, the ordered way of life as it had been, altered dramatically. Historical records, art, and culture, were of no value to the illiterate invaders, and became casualties in the assault. Many risked their lives to hide literary treasures away, or else we'd have nothing remaining of the great Greek thinkers and writers, and recorded history—the classics—as we know today. Even so, we possess little of the mountainous volumes that once were.

The world plunged into centuries of what we call, The Dark Ages—so named for the loss of life, culture, elevated arts, and broad spectrum literacy and learning. When the dust settled, the next generations began the arduous task of picking up the pieces. The church led the efforts to rebuild in the wake of great damage. New forms of governing replaced the old, giving rise to the feudal system with multiple kings and kingdoms.

Britain was defenseless once the Roman troops left the island, leaving them open to Viking invasion from the east and Irish raiders from the west. St. Patrick arrived on the scene in this season. A Roman-Brit kidnapped as a youth by Irish slave raiders, he eventually found freedom, returned to his homeland, and took service with the church. He was schooled in the classics and obeyed God's call to return to Ireland as an evangelist—the land where he'd been a slave.

When he stepped onto those green shores once

again, he brought with him the written Word of God—the Bible, and as many books of classic literary writings and culture that he could carry.

One by one, he taught anybody who wanted to learn. Surrounded by the glory of Creation in the Irish landscape, he helped people to "see and hear what we might pass by" through reflective learning. He told them stories—stories from the Bible. These stories stirred the hearts of the hearers to know more and to be able to read about it for themselves. By the end of his life, Patrick had revolutionized Ireland with the Gospel of Jesus Christ, literacy, and learning. The church flourished. His followers built places of learning known as monasteries, around which new villages and towns grew.

Some one hundred years later, St. Columba set off for the pagan Scottish shoreline with other missionaries, to evangelize and teach through story—dispelling darkness with the light of literacy. Imagine a great map of the region and those "lights" traveling southward throughout Scotland, as new believers grew and established monasteries where villages and towns rose-up around them. A light here—another there—and so forth throughout the lands heading south through Britain, and eventually across the channel into Europe, spreading the gospel and Christianity in every direction.

Lights in the Dark Ages through the power of story—His Story—burned bright as literacy and learning followed the path paved by God's Word.

But, many villages were difficult to reach. How might more lights be lit in the dark? The answer to this question brings us back to the beginning of this article.

Once upon a time in medieval Europe, storytellers roamed from village to village in colorful Pageant Wagons.

These horse-drawn, portable stages overflowed with all manner of costuming, masks, and props—the tools of the trade for the story merchant.

Pageant Wagons performed Miracle, Mystery, and Morality plays about the life of Christ, saints, and allegorical stories applying biblical principles in everyday life. For most, this was the only Bible to which the people of the day had access—acting out God's Word, learning to love the Lord and a literate lifestyle.

Professional actors, musicians, poets, and select clergy involved the whole population of the town in these colorful storytelling festivals. Men, women, and children of all ages freely participated in this interactive feast of entertainment and instruction, expressing the joy of creative living and lessons learned in God, good things, and beauty.

Just imagine it! When the Pageant Wagons rolled into town, the routine busy of all life stopped. Tradesmen closed-up shop, devoting all their energies to assist in the construction of staging, sets, costumes, and props, that could not be transported on the wagons. The entire village gathered, preparing food for one and all. Eager townspeople were swiftly schooled to act in some scenes. Soon the crowds assembled for the show.

Every day, in the middle of the day, under the light of the sun, the history of God's dealings with man, as outlined from Genesis through Revelations, was enacted with much fanfare. People who lived dull work rituals took a mental and spiritual vacation from the humdrum to stir rusty gears of thought and reasoning about important and life altering concepts—a retreat.

Retreat. Reflection. Rest. Renewal.

The desire to learn more, and grow into greater things, sparked within their hearts through the love of

God and liberty of His Truth. Their minds renewed—reset on higher things. The Pageant Wagon brought a ray of light and literacy into a dark and illiterate era of history. Restoring literacy to the people put the Word of God into the hands of hungry disciples of all ages.

Through the ministry of those Pageant Wagon storytellers, the foundation in Europe for the rebirth of literacy and learning we call the Renaissance was laid. The Renaissance laid the foundation for the Reformation, a world-changing light ignited by a learned priest named Martin Luther on October 31, 1517. One hundred years later, educated Christian pilgrims fled religious persecution in Europe to colonize the American shores, continuing the spread of literacy with the light of His Story, culminating in American independence.

Though peace continues to elude mankind in our present day, it's not for lack of light or literacy resources. It's how those resources are employed and the message they communicate that separates the Pageant Wagon storytelling of light, literacy, and hope, from platforms of deceptive, persuasive tales with dead ends.

It's exciting to be living in the middle of His Story in such times as these. The world appears to be in the throes of another barbarian invasion. Civilization is reaching a tipping point, threatening to plunge us, once again, into the Dark Ages. In these last days, more than ever, God surrounds us with His Presence calling us to Retreat to His Fragrant Fields.

Retreat to advance.

Stop to go forth.

Look to observe.

Listen to hear.

A Closing Word

In every glimpse of fragrant fields as you rush about your day; every bird-song heard joyfully declaring night dawning to light; every change of season marching onward, unflinching—He speaks. Hope. Selah.

You are called to Retreat.
Reflection. Rest. Renewal.
Romance. Restoration.

We impact the trajectory of a world filled with lost souls in need of Restoration when we allow spiritual Transformation in our own lives. We all have the power to be Pageant Wagons to the world. May you turn aside, face His Light, and choose daily to Rest in the Presence of our Lord on holy ground.

And the Angel of the Lord appeared to him in a flame of
fire from the midst of a bush.
So he looked, and behold, the bush was burning with
fire, but the bush was not consumed.
Then Moses said, "I will now turn aside and see this
great sight, why the bush does not burn."
So when the Lord saw that he turned aside to look,
God called to him from the midst of the bush and said,
"Moses, Moses!"
And he said, "Here I am."
Then He said, ". . . Take your sandals off your feet, for
the place where you stand is holy ground."
Exodus 3:2-5 NKJV

Earth is crammed with
Heaven!
Every bush is aflame
with the fire of God;
But only those who see it
take off their shoes.
The rest just pick the berries.

Elizabeth Barrett Browning

Notes

Noah Webster's 1828 Dictionary of the American English Language is available as a reference online: www.webstersdictionary1828.com

For an historical perspective on the Providential hand of God in preserving the church and His Word after the fall of Rome, and the impact of St. Patrick on safeguarding Western civilization for the purposes of God, refer to *How the Irish Saved Civilization* by Thomas Cahill.

For more information about Principle Approach Education ® and the Christian history of the United States of America, refer to the teaching and learning tools from the Foundation for American Christian Education online at www.face.net or the resources, books, and videos at www.wallbuilders.com.

About the Author

Kathryn "Miss Kathy" Ross, writer, speaker, and dramatist, ignites a love of literature and learning as a family through story and drama. Inspired by the stillness of birdsong, silent reflection, antiques, and teatime, she filters her love of history, classic literature, and the arts through God's Word, to inform her words. Old world elegance and a vintage hat distinguishes her captivating stage presence.

Trained in Principle Approach® Education through the Foundation for American Christian Education, Miss Kathy previously taught in Christian and homeschool settings, and provides enrichment programs in public schools. She specializes in writing and publishing curriculum tools for homeschoolers and church discipleship, promoting a Family Literacy Lifestyle—reading together, learning together, loving together—all ages, all at the same time.

Miss Kathy is the author/owner of Pageant Wagon Publishing. She designs story-worlds spanning the likes of an idyllic English country village to a Wild West gold rush town. In addition to her diverse inspirational speaking and teaching topics, she blogs and podcasts original works plus literacy related posts online at TheWritersReverie.com, and her publishing website at PageantWagonPublishing.com. Contact Kathryn Ross at info@pageantwagonpublishing.com to learn more about her speaking programs, availability, and fees.

More from
Pageant Wagon Publishing

Fable Springs Parables
High-concept Picture Books and Study Guides

Homeschool Enrichment and Theatrical Scripts
for Home, Schools, and Churches

Inspirational Christian Living
Devotionals for Journaling

*Pageant Wagon Publishing provides biblically based
storybooks, study guides, drama scripts, homeschool
enrichment, and devotional works to promote a
Family Literacy Lifestyle through Christian discipleship
for home, church, and classroom.*

Visit us online to order books
and learn more:
www.pageantwagonpublishing.com
Blogging at www.thewritersreverie.com

Made in the USA
Middletown, DE
15 May 2021

39605836R00066